WITCHES & WIZARDS

5

**Five Witches find
eternal wisdom**

PENFOLD BOOKS

Contents

Introduction

Towards the end of the 20th Century, disillusionment with materialism, politics and organised religion created a vacuum in the Western world. The scientifically objective age of logic and absolute truth gave way to the postmodern era, in which subjective experience took centre stage. Society, academia and the media began increasingly to look with tolerance and even favour on the mystical, with magic and witchcraft rising to new levels of acceptability in the public mind.

Witchcraft. The word breathes its own fascination. However, care is needed when defining terms. Followers of Wicca, or white witchcraft, claim to use 'white magic' for beneficial purposes only, such as healing, wholeness and prosperity. They maintain that their craft is innocent, natural and beneficial; not at all related to 'black witchcraft', which involves overtly negative practices, including the invocation of curses. Others claim the two crafts are more closely related than their practitioners admit.

In this unique book, five former witches, some white, some black, tell their true-life stories. This presents an opportunity not only to explore a fascinating world in which truth is often stranger than fiction, but also to uncover what lies behind this shadowy world of claim and counter claim.

Web of Light

by
Rachel Williams
England

Take your pick. The early morning autumn sunlight dancing with the mist of a forest of fading leaves; or a glorious rainbow arching over a mountain peak; or a golden sunset reflected in a glassy lake? From earliest childhood such scenes evoked in my heart a yearning for the magic of life – a merging of 'God and nature' that would fill my soul with wholeness and liberty.

Among a host of childhood memories, certain pivotal events stand out as having a distinct bearing on the dramatic course of my later life. At the age of six, kitted out in a pointed hat, cape and broomstick, I attended a Halloween party. The mystery and magic of that occasion remained with me ever after, igniting within me a desire to discover more of the fascinating world of ghosts and witches. Curiously, a few years later, in my school's end of term play, I starred as the witch in *Snow White and the Seven Dwarfs*. I relished the role and played it well enough that ever after my classmates called me 'witch'. Peer labelling affected me to the point where I began to act out that role on a daily basis, unconsciously taking on that identity in my mind.

I began noticing déjà vu experiences and eventually during my teenage years dabbled in the occult with some friends using a homemade ouija board. In 1973, at the age of fifteen, I chose to do a school topic on 'the supernatural'. Inspired by a series of articles on witchcraft in the *Sunday People* newspaper, I searched my local library, returning armed with piles of books on ghosts, witchcraft and the occult. I was impressed. A new world opened before my eyes. It gripped me and drew me in, eager to know and experience more. Around that time I bought a book on astrology at W.H. Smith's. Reading the stars quickly became an obsession with me.

At 17 I met a woman who called herself a white witch. She befriended me at a time of vulnerability due to my father's severe illness. She found work for me, and her kindness impressed me. As we became better acquainted, she began to use her psychic ability on me, telling me things about my life I felt she could not have known by natural means. On one particular visit to her house, she asked if I'd like to stay overnight. "Have you ever seen 'the light' when you've been meditating?" she enquired.

When I replied in the negative, she offered assistance. Hungry to learn anything 'new', I agreed to give it a try. She spoke softly as we began: "Imagine sunlight is rising through your body slowly reaching to the top of your head." Using 'creative visualization' I felt the light spiralling around me and a warm glow filling my being. I soon became visually aware of a radiant brightness. Such experiences thrilled me, uplifting my soul and giving purpose and meaning to my life.

My friend taught me all about 'chakras' – energy points apparently located at seven places in the body, beginning at the base of the spine and ending with the crown of the head. The sixth chakra (ajna), located in the forehead, is known commonly as the 'Third Eye'. Through further meditation techniques, I was encouraged to release 'kundalini' energy into my body to bring about oneness with the Divine. My friend told me that 'the light' I saw – call it spirit, Chi or just plain 'energy' – flowed through the seven chakras, forming a bridge to God. She used a pack of Tarot Cards to divine my past, present and future, while training me in the arts of divination, crystal healing and various areas of psychic gifting.

A Jewish girl joined us and for four years, almost on a nightly basis, we studied the occult arts. We began drawing up astrological charts for friends. 'Helping' people made me feel good about myself. I had esoteric knowledge and clients trusted me implicitly. I felt loved and accepted, receiving pleasing attention from admiring friends. The way also opened up for some media work, which in turn brought pop-stars and celebrities to our door in search of their futures.

I attended classes on 'spirit guides' and was introduced to entities claiming to be from North America and Medo-Persia. I developed as a Medium and was convinced that I could see the deceased relatives of my clients. One day I asked my spirit guide to take me to heaven, which led to a vivid spiritual experience in which I saw a beautiful city in the distance and two beautiful human-like angels standing looking at me. After this encounter I decided to switch from spirit guides to angels. I read all the 'angel books' I could find. Their purity attracted me as I searched for heavenly love and cleansing.

All continued serenely for more than a decade. But at the age of 33, my life fell apart. My partner, to whom I was engaged, left me for another woman. My fashion, music and advertising agency collapsed. Overwhelmed, I sought relief from my anguish and pain through my angels, crystals, self-help books and yoga. Nothing seemed to work. One day, lying on my bed, in deep emotional pain, I called out to God: "Father God, in heaven, I know that you're there, and that you can take me to heaven right now. I'm in so much pain and I know it's not your will for me to take my own life. So either take me to heaven or save me."

Why I prayed that prayer I cannot say. Perhaps the low point in my life brought back memories of my parents and the Bible class I had attended as a child. I did not become a Christian at that point, but God was at work behind the scenes.

As I lay there thinking, my mother telephoned to say that I should read Psalm 40. She had never suggested anything like this in my entire life. I dug out my childhood Bible – from among the shelves of books on the occult – and this (in part) is what I found:

"I waited patiently for the Lord; He turned to me and heard my cry.
He lifted me out of the slimy pit, out of the mud and mire;
He set my feet on a rock and gave me a firm place to stand.
He put a new song in my mouth, a hymn of praise to our God.
Many will see and fear and put their trust in the Lord.
Blessed is the man who makes the Lord his trust,
Who does not look to the proud, those who turn aside to false gods…
Do not withhold Your mercy from me, O Lord;
May Your love and truth always protect me.
For troubles without number surround me;
My sins have overtaken me, and I cannot see.
They are more than the hairs on my head,
And my heart fails within me.
Be pleased, O Lord, to save me;
O Lord, come quickly to help me."

How those verses touched me! For days I earnestly read the Bible, praying and crying to God. I knew I needed to attend a church meeting and hear the word of God preached, but I could not face it. Then I saw some meetings advertised in London near where I lived and, plucking up my courage, I went. The preacher spoke about a personal relationship with the Lord Jesus Christ. It wasn't what I expected. 'Church' to me was 'religion' – a system of rules and regulations – but how could a sinner like me ever keep it up?

Listening further, I quickly realised that I did not deserve God's mercy. My sins deserved the punishment of God in hell. My heart was broken and repentant. I was desperate for forgiveness and cleansing. I wanted to be saved from my sinful life and ungodly habits. When I heard that my creator, the Lord Jesus, had loved me so much that He had died for my sins on the cross, taking all the punishment I deserved on Himself, His love melted my heart. That day I repented of all my occult involvement, sin and rebellion against God, and I put my trust in Christ alone as Lord and Saviour. A while later I gathered together all my occult paraphernalia and burnt it (much to the amazement of my neighbours!).

The Lord saved me from the penalty, power and love of sin. He set me free from Satan's grip and gave me a whole new life with which to serve Him. Through the Lord Jesus I have experienced true joy, real peace and unfailing unselfish love. My guilty conscience has been cleared and my future is secure through the once-for-all perfect sacrifice of Christ on the cross, and His resurrection from the dead three days later.

As I look back, I see the frightening ease with which I was caught in a web of deception. Evil powers posing as 'positive energies' or highly evolved and beneficial beings, had lured me into the forbidden world of the occult. What I thought was light, actually turned out to be darkness. I found the Bible addressed this issue. "See to it, then, that the light within you is not darkness" (Luke 11:35); "…for Satan himself masquerades as an angel of light. It is not surprising, then, if his servants masquerade as servants of righteousness. Their end will be what their actions deserve." (2 Cor 11:14-15); "Woe to those who call evil good and good evil, who put darkness for light and light for darkness, who put bitter for sweet and sweet for bitter" (Isaiah 5:20).

It took me two years of walking with the Lord to free my mind of the false ideas and influences of my seventeen-year involvement in witchcraft. Today I rejoice in my wonderful Saviour, Jesus Christ, who has blessed me in so many ways and who has become "my light and my salvation." (Psa 27:1)

Shaman of the Rainforest

Elka
Guyana, South America

Elka, the witchdoctor, sat clutching his healing stones and blowing on the shivering body of a man wasted by a tropical disease. Focusing on the spirits of the forest pig, the humming bird, the jaguar and the anaconda, and beseeching their help, Elka looked down compassionately on his patient. Perhaps they would heal him: perhaps not.

At the age of ten he had watched Mafolio with awe, as he sought to heal his own stepfather with magic. Mafolio was the greatest and most highly respected witchdoctor in that part of the rainforest. Feared yet loved, he worked ceaselessly among the tribals, paddling his canoe up and down the rivers, seeking to cure the sick. Elka's desire to be a witchdoctor stemmed from that encounter.

The spirit 'Kworokyam' was central to the life of the Wai Wai tribe in British Guyana. A kind of composite of all the spirits of the forest, Kworokyam animated all life. A somewhat capricious deity, he would often strike with sickness and yet he was the same one to whom the witchdoctors prayed to heal the sick. Elka felt it was his task to extract 'the good' out of him. Others were not so well intentioned – like Muyuwa, a sinister figure from the other side of the mountain who worked dark magic for murderous purposes. A lustful witchdoctor, he stalked women at night, terrorising the whole countryside.

A vivid dream came to Elka in which he saw the spirits of a wild pig, a humming bird, a giant anaconda and an armadillo. "Sing the songs of Kworokyam," the pig said in a commanding tone.

Elka related the dream to Mafolio. "I heard him speak, but his throat never moved. Who was it that talked in the pig?"

"That was Kworokyam," explained Mafolio. "Kworokyam reveals himself to whom and in the way he wills. To you, Little Body, he is in the wild pig."

During another night the pig spirit visited Elka again. "I want you to be a witchdoctor," the creature, now part pig, part man, said to him. "Then you will not eat me, except for a tiny piece along my back. If you eat more of me than this, I will eat your spirit. If you neglect me, you will also die."

From that night on, Elka found himself being frequently contacted by the spirit world. He felt privileged. A real witchdoctor, who controlled the spirits and who was, in turn, controlled by them, was a rarity indeed. It entailed a mysterious life – a life to be dreaded. Cruel demands accompanied this calling – self sacrifice, wearisome journeys, long days and nights of blowing and the fear, even hatred, of the very people he felt led to serve.

Elka's uncle was a witchdoctor of some experience and took it upon himself to train his nephew. Together they erected a witchdoctor's hut. Here Elka would be transported to higher realms of the spirit world where he would learn the arts of healing magic. "Let your mind be filled with many spirits," his uncle counselled. "Not just with the bush hog, but with the anaconda, the vampire bat, the vulture and the haimara." The more 'pets' he possessed in the spirit world, the more Kworokyam would be pleased with him. The more songs he learned – one for each spirit – the more situations he could successfully navigate. For each animal spirit he took a smooth stone from the riverbed for use in healing ceremonies. He hoped Mafolio would pass on some of his stones, to make him an even more powerful healer.

"Take my tobacco. Crush it in your hand. Suck it in. Enjoy a tiny touch of Kworokyam," Elka's uncle instructed the people. Old and young pressed forward to taste the nectar of the gods. Two cheroots were lit and tobacco smoke was puffed into Elka's face for him to inhale. His initiating ceremony had begun. He coughed and spluttered.

"Don't sneeze," his uncle said sternly. "Swallow the breath of the spirits. To be a true follower of Kworokyam you must know him as well as you know people."

The time for Elka's 'journey to the sky' had arrived. Elka and his uncle entered the hut alone. "We'll sing more songs of Kworokyam. We'll sing to the humming bird, that most gracious of spirits, and she will come down and transport us both to the sky," said his uncle.

As they sang and smoked together, giddiness overcame Elka. His arms hung loosely at his sides. His head spun. He felt as if he were drunk. The light in the hut was dim. For Elka it grew dimmer and dimmer, until at last it went out.

When Elka recovered from his 'trip to the sky' he told the people what he had seen. "We saw people there, little people," he said. "Some had red skins, some black and some white. Clothes hid the bodies of others. I saw the anaconda and many bush hogs. The old snake and the pigs, my uncle said, would be my special pets."

While in his trance state, Kworokyam had 'taken over' his body, speaking through Elka's vocal chords. The words heard by the people outside were words that he had never used before, words he neither understood nor controlled. "I am a real witchdoctor now," he said aloud. "I will be a good witchdoctor who harms no one." Elka grew in stature as the years passed. His people esteemed him highly as a wise leader and a spiritual healer among his people.

News came from a tribesman up the river that strange white men had arrived. Previous explorations into the rainforest by white men had not been successful. Seen as a threat by the native Indians, they either went missing or were found dead, more often than not with their heads smashed open. However, these new reports told of white people who were caring and who had 'powerful healing magic' that had helped many of the people. They did not steal other men's wives, nor kill the natives. Elka and his people were intrigued. "They talk about God. But who is their God?" The Wai Wai tribe discussed among themselves. "Their God is not Mawalee who sprang from the union of the anaconda and the turtle. Neither is he Kworokyam. This God has no father or mother, just a Son called Jesus."

"I remember they said that men drove big nails through the Son's hands; spikes like those of the pimpler palm. They said that Jesus died because he wouldn't stop loving us," said one man who had heard the white men speak.

"How ever in the world could that be?" asked Tochi, looking up from her spindle. "What kind of love is that? Not Wai Wai love." She was right. The Wai Wai loved a child because someday he would grow up to hunt and cook meat for a parent. They loved selfishly – for what love could give. When other pressures entered, it was easy for 'love' to be swept away.

Soon after, a disease that caused bloated stomachs threatened tribal life. Many began coughing up blood. Muyuwa, the evil old witchdoctor teamed up with Elka. They worked side-by-side, smoking cheroots and blowing the clouds of smoke on to the hurting parts of their patients' bodies. At times they took magic stones out of their pouches and rubbed them on those who suffered. Sometimes they inserted small hollow sticks in the mouths of their patients in order to suck out the evil. All the while they sang songs to their animal spirits. Some recovered: however, many died. Then two white men appeared. They were known as Bahm and Mistokin. They administered medical tablets and injections. People began to recover dramatically. Elka watched the men very closely. He found them utterly mystifying. Often Elka had

12

yearned for high morals among the Wai Wai. However, while wife-swapping, orgies, drunkenness and stealing were commonplace among his own people, it was clear that Bahm and Mistokin lived lives of purity, even despite some of the tribal women flirting with them. Elka stood confronted by a different set of values. These men were different, not only in lifestyle but also in their message. They told of a creator God who was separate from the sun, moon and stars, the plants and the animals.

As the villagers sat with the white men and asked questions, the missionaries turned to their 'talking paper' to supply the answer. They called it the Bible. The missionaries talked straight. With the authority of God's paper, they spoke against many things no one had dared to challenge before. They said that God opposed the killing of innocent babies – and since the missionaries arrived the killings had stopped.

"God has revealed Himself to you by these trees, this river, the sky. Creation shows His power and wisdom," said Bahm, turning to the attentive Elka. "But you have turned your backs on Him. Instead of worshipping God, you have chosen to worship the things He has made. You are not alone in turning away from God. People in my own country have turned their backs on God too. In fact, I was once no different to you; then someone told me that despite my pride and rebellion, God had loved me and sent His only Son to die for my sins on the cross. I turned from my sin and believed alone in this Saviour as my Lord. Now I've come to tell you this message."

Some of the men, their consciences disturbed by the straight preaching, began to speak against the missionaries behind their backs and plotted to kill them. After one failed attempt, in which the tribals felt that the missionaries' God had protected them, they left the missionaries alone. Bahm and Mistokin continued to teach the Wai Wai about God's love for them and how he had proved it by giving His only Son as a sacrifice for their sin on the cross. They preached that the Wai Wai should turn from their sin and their idols, including Kworokyam, to the living Creator. The way to freedom from the spirit world, death and the 'badness within', was through the sinless atonement and resurrection of

God's unique Son. If they would bow to Jesus as Lord, they would receive everlasting life as a free gift.

A struggle commenced in Elka's soul. He felt drawn to this righteous yet loving God who was so utterly foreign to the Wai Wai's traditions. In his conscience he knew that he had *done wrong* and that *he was wrong* by nature. He had to admit he was ruled by fear of the spirits. What would happen if he rejected Kworokyam and followed the Lord Jesus? Would the spirits kill him as they had threatened? What would the people think if their respected witchdoctor gave up the tribal traditions?

He decided to believe in the missionaries' God *and* Kworokyam at the same time! God was good, he reasoned, and so was his practice of witchcraft. He had never hurt anybody (unlike Muyuwa). Yes! This was the solution to the problem – or so he thought.

A while later, Chiriminoso, another witchdoctor, organised a drinking party. During the dances the people imitated various animals and the men sought to prove their manhood by daring the drink to 'throw them'. Elka could not join in the drunken revelry due to a fever. Fearing he would die, he called on God: "Father in the Sky, this is old Elka talking. Would you be the one to heal me?"

When he recovered he wondered whether to give the credit to God or Kworokyam. He continued to use his tribal healing ceremonies until one tragic day when his own two-year old daughter fell so ill he thought she would die. Almost admitting the powerlessness of his craft again he called out to God: "Make my little girl well, Father. I want to be trusting in you."

Again his prayer was answered. His daughter recovered, but his practice of witchcraft continued – albeit without much, if any effect.

"The spirits used to honour my blowing," he said one day to Bahm. "Why don't they now?"

"The evil spirits sometimes seem to heal," Bahm answered, "But just to

14

fool us. Kworokyam is the Devil's servant. His 'healings' are just his way of keeping us in slavery to the evil spirits. God's paper tells us we cannot serve two masters. The Lord Jesus came to destroy the power of Satan. He came to release us from his power. If you receive the Lord Jesus, He will set you free from all that binds you. But you must choose – it's Christ or Kworokyam."

Requests from the tribe for Elka to use his powers showed no sign of drying up. Though he went into his hut to 'go to the sky', it no longer seemed to work. All the time he kept on thinking about what Bahm had said. Finally the battle came to a head. He sat down on a log and spoke to God: "Here I am, Father. I'm a witchdoctor. This is what I am. I'm a bad person, too. I get angry. I scold my wife. And I'm sad about those things. This is the way I don't want to be. So my old being, take it out, Father. You can because your Son died for my badness, to take it away. Make me to be another kind of person. I want to be like you."

In contrition, the young Indian bowed his black-crowned feather festooned head. One by one he named his sins: hatred, lust, envy and foolish pride. "This is the way I am, Father," he prayed quietly and sincerely. "Make me to be like Jesus. That is all I have to say."

That afternoon when he joined the others at the missionaries' hut, his heart was racing. Now he understood what Bahm and Mistokin had been saying. He saw everything through different eyes. The missionaries lived the way they did, not because of their own goodness, but through the power of the risen Lord living inside them. Peace, joy and assurance flooded Elka's soul.

As he lay in his hut that night, Elka thought about the box of charms above his head. He now knew that his witchcraft materials were an offence to God. Fear gripped him. Could he stand against the spirits and live? He remembered one witchdoctor who had thrown away his charms only to be mercilessly tormented by the spirits until he died one night, screaming in agony. Elka, trusting that Christ was stronger than Satan, resolved to throw away the tools of his craft. Muyuwa, the sorcerer, tried to persuade him not to do it, but Elka was resolute.

"Why are you going to throw away your charms?" asked the old witchdoctor.

"Because I want to," replied Elka.

"That is bad if you do that. A witchdoctor never stops being a witchdoctor, unless he wants to die."

"But I have accepted the Lord Jesus," said Elka. "I have received Him in truth. For this reason I want to throw away my charms. I won't die. God will protect me."

"Save one charm, just one – to protect yourself," the old man pleaded.

"If I hold back even one it will be bad to God. So I want to give them all up," came Elka's answer. Muyuwa sat down on a rock in the shade of a tree with Elka squatting alongside him.

"It's like this," he said, trying to get through to the old, hardened mind. "If the spirits kill me, don't believe in the Lord Jesus. If I live, you must become His companion."

Surrounded by onlookers, Elka disposed of his charms, publicly renouncing witchcraft. Some tried to stop him, fearful that the spirits would kill him, but with a smile on his face and with great calm, he put his life in God's hands. Thus in 1954, this witchdoctor became a disciple of Jesus.

Days became weeks and ran into months. Elka did not die, but grew in his faith. He was keenly watched. If he could break free from Kworokyam, why not others? When the people saw him eat, without harm, the meat of a pig that the spirits had prohibited, many realised that Jesus Christ truly had power over Kworokyam. Many became Christians. Even Muyuwa, the dark sorcerer, received Christ, along with several other witchdoctors.

Thus began a new day for Elka and his people the Wai Wai, as they discovered the joy, peace and forgiveness of God. Freedom in Christ. Liberty from the spirits. Yet the story had only just begun, for the Wai Wai believers became intrepid missionaries to other tribes in the rainforest, proclaiming God's love and the gospel of light to them.

Egyptian Magic

by
Lloyd Paul Gallimore
London, England

The pathways of life are marked by many twists and turns, but surely none is calculated to alter one's perspective and destiny like the scourge of child abuse. Such was my case in 1967, at the age of nine. It left me feeling utterly unclean inside. This much I knew – I could not tell anybody. My answer to the pain, guilt and humiliation was to isolate myself and seek inner spiritual healing, even at such a young age. All alone for long periods, I began to sense spiritual presences in my room and felt I could actually see spirits.

Knowing my mother was a deeply spiritual woman, I confided in her. "Well Lloyd, I wondered when this kind of thing would come out in my children. You see, I come from a long line of tarot card readers and psychic healers." That day I felt a sense of destiny. Perhaps my life would amount to something after all. It appeared an entire spiritual world was opening up before me – waiting to be explored.

My father was employed as a curator in the Greco-Roman Antiquities section of the *British Museum*. He returned from work one day with a book about ancient Egyptian civilization, which included a section on 'The Egyptian Book of the Dead'. The mystery and excitement of the unknown grew within me as I pondered the chapter. I soon became hooked on books about the supernatural and, though only a child, had soon exhausted my local library's occult and paranormal section.

At the age of 13 I made contact with my first spirit guide. It appeared unexpectedly and told me to fetch a pen and paper. I felt empowered as another entity worked through me, enabling me to draw with a degree of skill far above my natural abilities. Around this time I joined a Kung-Fu club. My martial arts teacher happened to believe in the spiritual and philosophical side of the sport and told me that spirit guides were necessary if I wanted to make progress.

I committed myself to greater involvement in all things spiritual. I took up yoga, Tai Chi and other disciplines. I sought instruction from my spirit guides and the writings of occultic authors. Peace, joy and oneness with the universe seem to fill my life. I learned to deal with negative energies like guilt and fear by focusing instead on positive energies such as love and peace. My mind, body and spirit felt balanced and in tune with the elements: earth, air, wind and fire.

My love of books led me from library to library. I studied Taoism, Zen Buddhism and Feng Shui. I practiced I Ching, astrology and tarot and regularly attended the *Mind, Body and Spirit Festival* at Earls Court. I bought literally hundreds of books on occult related subjects and was a regular customer at *Atlantis* and *Watkins*, two famous occult bookstores in London's West End, where I discussed my interests with the staff. Carlos Castaneda's books influenced me a great deal, but I refused to take drugs because I wanted a clear mind. By the age of 18, people were coming to me for tarot readings and asking for spiritual advice. In my own way I had become something of an expert and showed considerable psychic ability.

At that time I qualified as a library assistant at the *British Library*. This was a paradise for me − row upon row of occult books! Every spare minute was spent increasing my knowledge of the esoteric. While there, I met a serious witchcraft researcher. As I unearthed rare books for her, at times I found her requests were denied because she wanted books in the 'unclassified' section. This inadvertently led me to a real treasure chest. I began to study books on deep magic and witchcraft that were unavailable to the public. There were many such books, including some ancient handwritten copies.

The lady visitor and I met regularly for coffee to chat about witchcraft. She introduced me to the works of some of the founders of the New Age Movement, like Madame Blavatsky and Alice Bailey. I completed a course in the *National Federation of Spiritual Healers*. It turned out that she was a white witch who belonged to the *Temple of Isis*. This Egyptian branch of magic and witchcraft fascinated me, so, at her invitation, I joined her occultic house group. There we studied magic, occult ritual, Tantric sex and witchcraft, chanting and calling up spirit beings from ancient Egypt.

One night, at a house in London, while calling up Egyptian deities, the witches summoned Anubis. When it came, it possessed me. I became like a dog, barking, howling and growling. There was nothing they could do to help me. It appeared they had invoked a spirit they could not control. After this experience I left the group and entrusted myself to my spirit guides – I felt much safer in their hands.

Soon after this I met a woman who worked for a national newspaper who was heavily involved with voodoo and black magic. After living with her for a year and allowing her to practice love-binding spells and magic on me, I left. She had been with other men behind my back. The night before leaving, she attempted to call up demons in order to hold me prisoner to her will.

In 1988, while still at the *British Library*, I met a very unusual woman. She requested books on the goddess Sekhmet, the most important of Egypt's leonine deities. She was about five feet tall, half Tibetan, a student at *Cambridge University* and clearly a very serious student of the occult. When we eventually became friends, she told me she was searching for a particular amulet, but would not tell me which one. Since I owned an amulet bearing an image of Sekhmet, guessing it might be what she was looking for, I gave it to her. She claimed it was the very one for which she had been searching – and that this signified that I should be her scribe, to record messages from the spirits.

The two of us met regularly to worship at her shrine to Egyptian deities in her home. She often visited the *British Museum*, which in those days was next door to the *British Library*, to worship the gods in the Egyptian section first thing in the morning. For two years when we met together, frequently a spirit would inspire me to write messages sometimes in English, other times in Sanskrit – a language she knew but I didn't. One day all I wrote was a single word, which neither of us recognised. Checking at the library, it turned out to be the Hebrew word *Yahweh*, one of God's names in the Old Testament. This strange event piqued my interest, not in Orthodox Judaism or Christianity – both of which I considered narrow-minded and backward – but in the Jewish Cabbalistic writings. During my research into Cabbalism I had a Jewish spirit guide who, in my eyes, seemed far wiser and purer than all my previous guides, which led me to remove all the idols from the shrine in my house.

Despite my wide knowledge and experience in the occult and the fact that I was a leading white witch, I was beginning to notice some negative side effects. The powers that worked through me had grown so strong that I had become unable to control them. I would suddenly start prophesying or predicting the future during work, which unnerved people around me. I became increasingly disturbed and obsessive. I started to give away all my possessions and made a prediction that I would die the following Christmas Day.

My sister, who had become a Christian, had been praying for me; so had her whole church. Alarmed at my deterioration, she asked her Minister to visit me. I was deliberately rude to him, even quoting Bible verses at him to drive him away. It worked, because he left, apparently not knowing what to do with me. I had no time for these weak Christians. Pitiful, yet sincere, I knew they were utterly deluded. I laughed when they gave me 'scary' warnings about the occult. They obviously didn't know that I, as a white witch, was protected by an aura of positive energy. Anyway, they were so woefully ignorant they did not even understand the difference between Wicca and black magic – they simply condemned it all as 'evil witchcraft'.

Christmas Day came. As the family gathered at the table and bowed their heads to say 'grace', I began frantically and uncontrollably 'predicting the future'. It was an unmitigated disaster. As for my untimely death – the spirits were obviously wrong, for nothing happened.

I began to show symptoms of schizophrenia. Sometimes I wandered aimlessly through the streets for hours at a time. I refused all offers for help. About this time, my spiritual activities came to a head. While staying with my brother, late one night during a thunderstorm I put on some occult music and called up demons using a book on black magic. I felt driven to do this from within. It was as if I had been taken over and had become a helpless victim. As I shouted for Lucifer himself to come and be with me, my brother was so scared that he locked himself in his room. Apparently the noise of this whole episode disturbed the neighbours because the Police were called and took me to a psychiatric hospital ward at Greenwich where I was diagnosed with hypermania.

I spent the next nine months on drugs to keep me calm. I do not remember much that happened but I know that when I was released I ended up in a hostel. My family invited me to church to watch my dad and mum get baptised. Apparently my dad had become a committed Christian – which shocked me. Despite many attempts to convert me, I refused to accept Christ and claimed I was a Buddhist. Yet my curiosity led me to a serious investigation of the Bible. I spent two years reading it from cover to cover, looking for answers. I also read several good Christian books, one of which gave Biblical explanations about the dangers of the occult. The light was beginning to dawn. I was being challenged to rethink my position.

One night, in 1991, as I read the Bible (in 1 Thess 4:3-8) God spoke to me about my sinfulness. For the first time in my life, I realised the dreadfulness of my sin against God. It was a dark and solemn moment. I was lost – and deservedly on my way to an eternal hell. Yet, in His marvellous grace, God revealed to me that night how the Lord Jesus, God's unique Son, had come into the world to save sinners like me. It dawned on me that His death on the cross and his resurrection were God's way of bringing me salvation. Falling to my knees, I owned my guilt and repented of my sin, putting my trust alone in the Lord Jesus. I received Christ and rejected Satan. I even read out a kind of church creed saying that I rejected the devil and all his works. For the first time in my life I felt holy and clean.

As I learnt more and more of God's word, with the help of the dear Christians who counselled me, I began to grow in faith. I burnt over 1,000 occult books! Despite periods of intense struggle during which I felt Satan trying to pull me back, through the power of Christ I was constantly delivered from the powers of darkness. My depression lifted, enabling me to come off the tablets. I even felt able by the Lord's grace to put my childhood abuse behind me.

The Christian life is not a bed of roses. It is tough and approaches life's difficulties differently. Previously, when faced with a problem, I used to try and focus on positive energy and brush any negative energy under the carpet. Now I face up to the negative and experience God's power and grace in repentance, forgiveness and holiness.

For 24 years I absorbed myself in white witchcraft. In all sincerity I thought I was 'doing good'. I believed that white magic was the good side of 'the force' – black magic the bad side. Now I realise that both are from Satan, like two sides of the same coin. Lucifer is a deceiver who works through a host of evil spirits to trick people into counterfeit experiences of spirituality. All the time I thought I was receiving more light and greater psychic powers, in reality I was being filled with darkness. How wonderful it is now to be filled with God's light – the light of the knowledge of the glory of God in the face of Jesus Christ.

Dancing with Darkness

by
Audrey Harper
London, England

"I served Satan as a loyal and willing member of a black magic coven, and kept my secret for 25 years. I often wanted to tell, but did not dare. In the early stages, I was afraid for myself. Later, I was afraid for my family. I was afraid people simply would not believe me. When I did finally tell what I had seen, it was to an audience of millions watching a TV show.

"Judging by the response, my few, carefully chosen words had quite an impact. The press were knocking at my door and my name was in the headlines. I did not want publicity, but I suppose it is not every day somebody goes before the cameras and reveals that she has witnessed the murder of a baby in a witchcraft ceremony, or that some witches covens are financed by the sale of pornographic photos taken at child abuse parties.

"I had been carrying the awful secret far too long. It had haunted my sleep and almost driven me crazy with worry. Now I was glad it was out in the open. It was not a pretty story, as you will soon discover, but it had to be told."

Thus begins Audrey Harper's account of her life in witchcraft. How did she ever become involved in the first place? Like many practitioners of Satanism and Black Magic, she experienced rejection and emotional pain in childhood. Born on Christmas Day 1939, she was packed off to a *Dr. Barnardo's Home* because her mother could not cope with yet another baby. Desperate for love and a sense of belonging, she was always going to be a vulnerable target.

On leaving School at 18, she joined the *Women's Royal Air Force* in Cheshire, England. Posted to *RAF Halton* in Buckinghamshire to receive basic nursing training, she fell in love with David. For the first time in her life she felt someone cared for her. David was appointed to work in Bahrain and just before he left, he gave Audrey a beautiful diamond ring. During David's absence, Audrey discovered she was pregnant with his child. When David heard, he was so excited that he immediately arranged to return home. He never arrived. His plane crashed on its way to England. In her grief Audrey turned to drink. As a result she was unable to properly care for her son after he was born. Put up for adoption, her baby was taken away. She never saw him again.

Audrey's life was spiralling downwards. In desperation she went to London and lived on the street, turning to prostitution and theft to pay for her drug and alcohol addictions. Then a chance meeting in her favourite pub just off Curzon Street changed her life forever. In her own words:

"One night I caught the eye of two women who had been looking at me. They were well-dressed, both in their early thirties, nicely made up with expensive hairdos. At first I thought they were brass, high-class, not like me. But there was something about them that made them stand out from the other customers – some quality I sensed but could not define.

"I got into conversation with them. They were swish and assured – and generous. They gave me cigarettes and bought me drinks, and, after some chatter, they invited me to a party to be held a few days later in Chelsea."

At the party, Audrey asked the women how they could afford such a sumptuous lifestyle. "All of this is available to anyone who really wants it. How badly do you want it?" they asked.

"Very badly," said Audrey, stuffing a sandwich in her mouth. "I'm fed up with scratching around for money. I can't even afford a proper place to live."

"There is a way for you to get absolutely anything you want – everything you ever dreamed of," the women insisted, inviting her to another party in Fulham. Audrey showed interest in their claims about power and wealth.

"A group of us meets every month in a place called Virginia Water," said one of the women. "We've been watching you – we think you'd fit in nicely. But you can't just walk in and join. You've got to be initiated. It's all very secret. You'll have to swear never to tell a soul."

"When do I come?" Audrey blurted out.

"October 31st – Halloween night," was the quick reply.

Diana and Shirley met Audrey at the station at Virginia Water. After a meal and a bath at Diana's luxurious house, Audrey was asked to put on a white robe. A chauffeur driven car pulled up. The blindfold Audrey had to wear during the journey was removed once inside the building. In Audrey's words:

"The building was obviously purpose-built. There was an altar at one end, and the altar cloth, purple in colour, had a golden pentagram emblazoned on it. There was another pentagram, much larger, set in tiles on the floor. There was very little light – just two black candles, flickering at either side of the altar. A heady, sickly-sweet smell from burning incense filled the room. The place was warm and there was a heavy air of expectancy. It took a little while to make out what was happening. There were a lot of shadowy figures around, between twenty and thirty altogether, all of them in hooded robes. Eleven of them were standing in a semi-circle facing the altar, with a gap in the middle. The others were standing behind. Later I found out why – the eleven were members of the coven I was to join, thus making up the twelve. The others were guests from other covens who had been invited along – an initiation on Halloween night is an important function."

What followed is too horrific to describe in detail. The chanting of the witches finally reached fever pitch. The High Priest summoned Audrey, asking her whether she desired initiation and if so, whether she promised to obediently serve her master at all times. Audrey assented. The High Priest cut her arm with a sacrificial knife and made her sign a covenant in her own blood declaring Satan her only master. A baby girl was brought in by her own mother and the High Priest slit its throat as a sacrifice to Satan. The blood was poured into a chalice and drunk by the covens. Then the High Priest ritually raped Audrey on the altar. The ceremony over, she was told that she would be contacted again. The covens quietly disbanded.

The following morning after a fitful night's sleep she hitched a lift to the Thames Embankment. Strolling along by the river she says: "Several times on the journey, and when I was walking along by the Thames, I pinched myself and wondered had it really happened? Had a baby really been murdered? Had I really been raped? Or was it all some dreadful nightmare, perhaps a trip after popping some of the hallucinatory pills I sometimes took? I'd like to think it hadn't happened. But it had. The memory was so fresh it hurt. Those hymns to Satan that the witches had sung so enthusiastically were still ringing in my ears.

"As the day progressed, I was gripped by more ominous thoughts. These people were powerful. They could harm anyone who threatened them or put a curse on anyone who failed to carry out their will. It occurred to me that I might be in danger. What could I do? Going to the police would be a waste of time. The Coppers knew me – a young junkie who had often been warned for soliciting. Would they believe me if I told them I had seen a baby having its throat slit? I doubt it. How much notice would they take if I reported a man in a long black cloak had raped me? Not very much. The more I thought about it, the more I came to realise I was trapped. In my head I had this frightening, dangerous knowledge, but the only people I could share it with were my fellow witches. Yes, my fellow witches: I was one of them now, and there was no escaping that fact.

"But it wasn't just that people might not believe me that stopped me telling. If these witches could show me the path to power and money, the last thing I wanted to do was to destroy them. Even though their evil deeds had shocked and disgusted me, I had gone there as a willing participant. One night, three or four weeks afterwards, I got a sudden blinding headache. It just wouldn't go away, whatever I took for it. I tried lying on the bed in Molly's flat, but the fierce pain persisted, like a pneumatic drill biting into my brain. Then came a voice telling me to be at Highgate Cemetery just before midnight. I tried not to listen. I did my best to get to sleep. But the headache persisted, and so did the voice in my mind. It was so insistent that I got up, got dressed, and caught the tube to Highgate.

"I had never been to Highgate or the cemetery before. I didn't even know of it, even though it is famous as Karl Marx's burial place. I didn't know the way when I got off the train – but I didn't need to ask. The voice gave me directions and, just before midnight, I found myself at the cemetery gates, called there by the witches. I wasn't the only one. There were a number of figures huddled round the gates. We trooped through the vast graveyard making our way to a corner area. I recognised some of the witches from Virginia Water. The warlock was there – I'd hardly be likely to forget him – and so was Mary, the mother of the sacrificed baby. Diana and Shirley, the pair who had met me at the station were there. Altogether, I'd say there were between thirty and forty of us. That night various incantations were recited and assorted occult rites observed."

At other meetings the witches practised casting spells, 'levitating', calling up spirits and developing psychic powers. Audrey was eventually given an organisational task within the coven. Instructed to invite teenagers to a party, she imagined her fellow witches wanted to teach a few occult methods to some potential new recruits. Nothing had prepared her for the shock that awaited her.

"Diana, who gave me my instructions, was quite specific about numbers, ages and sexes. I had to find about twenty people, mostly girls but some boys, aged between thirteen and eighteen. For somebody who knew London as well as I did, the job presented no difficulties. There were dozens of kids hanging around the cafés, amusement arcades and railway stations, many of them runaways who would readily go anywhere for a few free drinks and the promise of a wild night out."

That night some of the covens spiked the teens' drinks, causing them to let go of all restraint. It wasn't long before an orgy was taking place. Two of the witches started taking pictures. Audrey was disgusted:

"I felt sick – so sick in fact, that I had to leave. My head was reeling. I leaned against the wall in the hallway for support. Apparently this was how the coven made its money. There are people in all levels of society that will pay a lot of money for sexually explicit pictures of youngsters. Amazing but true. It may seem ironic that I, a prostitute, should have high principles about commercial sex. Sex among adults was one thing. But corrupting youngsters with drugs and using them for pornography was, to my mind, quite different. I found it appalling, and I resolved I would never have anything to do with it.

"Alas, other people had different ideas. When I made my 'moral' views known at the next gathering, the warlock fixed me with a long and angry glare. 'You don't own yourself any more,' he said. 'You belong to us. You belong to Satan. You will carry out his wishes.' As he spoke, he drew the athame (ritual knife) from beneath his cloak. I felt then that if I continued to refuse, he would kill me with as little compunction as he had slit that baby's throat."

For a time Audrey had to be the partner of the warlock and through him she learnt deeper occult techniques. She also became pregnant with his child. Fearing that the child might be sacrificed to Satan, she left the coven and had the child in a hospital but gave it up for adoption. Living with such dark secrets took its toll.

By 1963, she had become heroin dependant. To escape she fled to Southend to begin a new life. She even had a job for a while, but it didn't last. She soon slipped back – back to London, to heroin, prostitution, crime and the coven. A chance meeting brought a ray of hope into Audrey's ruined life. She met a kindly policeman who paid a court fine for her and invited her to his house. Chris and Ann his wife were a lovely couple. The home was like an oasis of love and acceptance. Over breakfast she asked, "Why did you do it Chris?"

Putting down his knife and fork, Chris paused, looked up and said: "I did it because I am a Christian. We want you to know that you can stay with us just as long as it takes to sort yourself out."

Audrey was stunned. "I had never encountered genuine goodness like this before, and I kept asking myself: 'What's their angle?' I couldn't understand it but I liked it. Here were people not just spouting from a pulpit, but also living their Christianity. I really admired them. I suppose it was the first time I had seen God's love in action. Chris said God would speak to me if I would be prepared to listen, but I was dismissive. Why should God speak to me? Why should God bother with someone who had signed up with Satan? Looking back, I realise this would have been the perfect opportunity to break away from the coven. Chris and Ann were both strong in their faith. They could have helped and protected me; but I didn't give them the chance."

After five days, Audrey's insatiable desire for drugs drew her back to the coven and her ambivalent relationship with heroin. She resumed her task of supplying kids for the immoral purposes of the avaricious witches' coven. During this time she met other Christians; worthy souls whose 'work for the Lord' brought them onto the streets to show genuine compassion to the likes of Audrey. There was the Salvation

Army officer at their centre in Soho. He was a kindly man who listened with great patience and offered to help Audrey get off drugs. He pointed her to Christ as the answer. Then there were the Christians at the Congregational Church in Orange Street who tried to get through to her in their coffee bar. "Members of the church used to mingle with us and try to share their Christian beliefs," she recalls. "I remember one of them saying to me: 'You don't have to live this way. Jesus can save you from drugs. The power of God can change your life.'

"They were kind, and they knew how to talk to young people without being patronising or forceful. I listened to bits of it, but I tended to think: 'It's all right for you, but you haven't been where I've been. You're not worried about where the next fix is coming from.' They were loving, caring people, and I tried to listen to them, but deep down I didn't really believe they could help me. Despite their assurances to the contrary, I thought my sins were too many and too bad for Jesus to even bother with me."

While in a drug unit for psychiatric patients in Tooting Bec, Audrey heard that a man called Frank Wilson ran a project called *Life for the World* designed to help addicts to break free. She contacted him and he came to see her in hospital. He took her home to be with his family for the weekend and on another occasion she went along with him to hear the evangelist Eric Hutchins. During this meeting, the preacher's message began to really hit home. He spoke about the mercy and grace of the Lord Jesus and His willingness to die for sinners – to forgive and make them whole. Audrey knew that she was a sinner, but she thought it was impossible to break free from the chains of her sin.

At the end of the service some former drug addicts went to the front to speak about how God had delivered them and given them new lives through Christ. Her hope was kindled and she prayed: "God, if you're there, you save me. If you really love me, you show me that you love me. If you really are who these people say you are, then you show me a new life. All right, then God. This is Audrey speaking. You have me. Go on, take me, all of me, rotten bits and all, and you show me that you love me."

God's love had already been unmistakeably at work in Audrey's life, but she still had a long way to go. Unbelief in the word and power of God held her back from blessing. Then there were the demons that controlled her. They weren't about to let her go without a fight. Frank helped her by putting her up with a loving Christian family, but despite these clear evidences that God was indeed being very gracious to her, the power of Satanism and the drugs proved too strong yet again. She ran away from the family.

Once, while searching for a pub, she heard music coming from a building and went in – only to find it was a church! Two old ladies took an interest in her and, finding out she was a drug addict, pointed her in the direction of a Christian rehabilitation farm in Redditch, Worcestershire. This proved a major turning point in her life. She not only came off drugs, but also met and married a man called John. They moved into a three-bedroom house in Droitwich. In 1973, Audrey gave birth to a baby daughter, whom they named Elizabeth.

Even though her life had changed in many ways, Audrey was still tormented by her dark secrets. If the family attended church, feelings of nausea would come over her. At times she wanted to curse and swear during the singing. She had donned the outward insignia of Christianity but inwardly she was a prisoner of Satan. The elders of the church sensed there was something seriously wrong and decided to approach Audrey. A volcano erupted in her heart:

"My feelings towards the church were murderous. I didn't just want to see their building burn down – I wanted to strike the match, preferably with all of them inside. My mind was in such a turmoil that I actually sat down and plotted to do this dreadful deed, much as I had plotted to kill my mother years before. Something had to give. I took an overdose."

John found Audrey in time to rush her to hospital. In hospital the battle raged on. She felt the voice of Satan saying: "You should know better than to try and get away from me. We made a deal and you've got to stick to it." Out of hospital and back in church services again, she had to take valium to stop herself cursing and throwing the communion wine over everyone.

One night, Roy Davies, a young preacher from the church was able to get close to Audrey. He said: "I am going to ask God what is wrong, and what can be done to put it right." He knelt down and prayed, and then very discerningly yet gently he said: "You've been involved in witchcraft, haven't you, Audrey?"

"I started crying," recalls Audrey. "For me that was rare. I'd had a pretty hard upbringing without much time for tears – but now I was sobbing uncontrollably. Then I realised Roy was crying with me." After pouring out the details about her life in witchcraft, Roy arranged to meet with her for prayer with several others. During the three-day wait, Audrey was tormented by evil thoughts and nightmares. Finally the meeting took place.

"Just what happened during the three hours I do not know," says Audrey. "It remains a blank in my mind."

"Until I met Audrey," Roy explained, "I had never had to deal with a case in which the demon spirits were so well established. They had occupied her soul for close on a quarter of a century. There are some people who cannot, or will not, accept that demon spirits can occupy a mind. They think that every person whose behaviour is erratic, irrational or downright evil is simply mentally disturbed. They are wrong. I have come across many people who are, to a greater or lesser degree, mentally unbalanced, even insane. There's a difference between insanity and demon possession. Surgery, drugs or psychoanalysis could never have cured Audrey's problem. It was definitely a spiritual issue. The demons must have felt they had right of tenancy in Audrey."

Audrey finally faced up to the sins that had been the manifestation of a heart not right with God. She was filled with an all-engrossing sense of her sin as being against God. She repented of her witchcraft, theft, blasphemy, rebellion, immorality, wilfulness and unbelief. The believers prayed for her deliverance. There was a mighty struggle – she reacted violently and strange sounds came from her body. She seemed in agony, her face all contorted – but that day the power of God set her free. Roy remembers:

"There was a feeling of relief when Audrey was able to make her final confession with real joy – that Jesus Christ was Lord, and that His blood had cleansed her completely." Audrey repented and believed in the Lord Jesus Christ, the Saviour who had died for her on the cross and risen again from the grave the third day.

To publicly declare her allegiance to Christ and obey His command, Audrey was baptised by immersion on March 23rd 1986. It was a day of unspeakable joy and victory – a day none of the people who had witnessed to her about the Saviour had ever dared to really imagine would come. Audrey's conversion from the power of Satan to God gives proof of the Bible text which declares, "The things which are impossible with men are possible with God" (Luke 18:27).

Today Audrey works full time helping people leave occultism. Knowing how easy it is to be drawn into Satan's web and how difficult it is to break free, she warns, "Steer clear of all kinds of witchcraft, and everything and anything to do with the occult."

Queen of the Black Witches

by
Doreen Irvine
London, England

1939 in the East End. Not a time and place many would choose to be born and raised – but such was the lot of Doreen Irvine. Family circumstances and World War 2 meant poverty and hardship for the young girl. Bad company and minimal parental guidance found her working as a prostitute in her teens, earning the nickname 'Daring Diana' at a strip club in Soho.

While there Doreen met two girls who made no secret of their Satanism. Doreen was fascinated with their conversation and soon counted them as her best friends. Desiring to learn as much as possible about black witchcraft, she was taken to a satanic meeting. Over 500 people were gathered that night. She witnessed various satanic rituals, including the sacrifice of a white cockerel. After the two hours she noticed the chief Satanist looking intensely at her. Doreen recalls:

"I was rather flattered when the chief Satanist asked me to join him for a meal. I felt a little nervous so he tried to put me at ease. It was not long before I found myself telling him my life story. He did not seem in the least bit shocked when I told him I was a drug addict, prostitute, and strip-tease artiste. Indeed, he seemed to know all about me.

Probably one of the girls I had seen in the club had put him in the picture. 'All kinds of people are Satanists,' he said. 'From the high to the low – bankers, shopkeepers, teachers, nurses, prostitutes, drug addicts. There's no difference between us. We are here to promote Satan on the earth whenever and however we can.'

"He had a strong personality and had no difficulty in persuading me to become a Satanist and his mistress. I was taught that evil – as most people think of evil – is not wrong, but right (and wholesome). It sounded stupid to me, as indeed it is, but I started to believe it. The Satanists twisted and distorted everything. A lie, I was told, was in fact the truth. All very confusing, but many believed it – even intelligent people. It was a kind of brainwashing. If you are told the same thing over and over again, you finally come to believe it, no matter how stupid it sounds."

At a larger meeting she sold her soul to Satan in a blood sacrifice. "I was sworn in as high priestess, a high honour indeed in Satanist circles. When I protested that I wasn't ready for such a place of honour, the chief Satanist said it was a request of the great Lucifer himself, and he must be obeyed. In this position I could serve my master better. I was qualified to handle the sacred vessels and wait at the high altar. I was known as the great priestess Diana. I felt very important – from a simple conversation overheard at the strip club I had now become a leader in Satanism, and Satan was indeed my master."

Doreen also joined a coven of black witches where she went even deeper into the occult than at the Satanist temple. She recalls: "All meetings included awful scenes of perverted sexual acts. Sex plays an important part in witchcraft. Sadism was practised frequently. Some even cut themselves with knives and felt no pain. My powers as a black witch were great, and I added to my knowledge of evil every day. Demons aided me. I practised more wickedness in a single week than many would in an entire lifetime."

Doreen progressed rapidly in witchcraft, eventually competing in a European contest for the title of Queen of the Black Witches on

Dartmoor. She recounts: "The scene was set for the great ceremony at which the next Queen of Black Witches was to be chosen. Black witches from all parts of England assembled, as well as witches from Holland, Germany and France. They arrived before Halloween, when Dartmoor became a hive of activity. After the rituals the great test of power began. Seven witches, including myself, were competing for the title. Success would not be easy, for these witches all had similar powers. Various supernatural feats were performed that eerie night on Dartmoor."

"Hail, Diana, Queen of Black Witches!" rose the loud cry of over a thousand witches, as Doreen triumphed. Following her coronation, Doreen and her chief Satanist lover travelled across Europe in luxury to visit other covens. She says: "Many discussions were held, the most important subject being how to make black witchcraft more appealing. Many people, especially the young, were taking a fresh interest in the occult. A successful marketing strategy depended on giving witchcraft a new look, so the following loose guidelines were laid down:

1. Offer new realms of 'mystery and excitement'.
2. Make witchcraft appear generally less sinister.
3. Give it the feel of a natural, innocent adventure.
4. Package evil in appealing wrappers.

"New recruits were needed if evil was to triumph. Time was short. Now was the time to trap people. Once people were involved in witchcraft, fear would hold many back from retreating. There would be no way out. We witches were devoted to our cause, dedicating our lives to the promotion of the occult.

"Back in England, much of my time was spent visiting covens. Many new ones were springing up and it was important to encourage new members. White witches were swelling the ranks and we learned from them. Although they claimed never to harm anyone, I knew some who did. Rituals involving dolls, which we called voodoo, white witches also practised, using a 'fith fath', a doll made of clay in the image of the person they wish to harm."

After a year in her role as Queen of the Black Witches, Doreen voluntarily stepped down but continued to pursue her worship of Satan at the temple in London. She says:

"Perhaps my greatest power was my ability to deceive. No one, besides the Satanists, knew of my darker activities – not even the man I lived with. I lived such a lie, such a double life, that not one soul ever suspected any of my satanic connections. Anyway, if I had told 'the truth' no one would have believed it.

"Throughout these years I had one mounting fear – that of growing old and dying. As the fear grew, so questions arose in my mind. Was hell the wonderful place I had been led to believe? Suppose it was just the reverse. What then? Since the doubts persisted and deepened, I began to think the unthinkable – could I break away? As far as I knew, no one had ever left black witchcraft – ever."

In 1964, Doreen went to a Christian meeting at Colston Hall, Bristol, to listen to an evangelist preach about Jesus Christ. She had seen posters around the town advertising the meeting for several weeks. Whenever she saw them, she ripped them down. Her one purpose was to attack the preacher.

The night began with someone singing a beautiful song about the Lord Jesus as a friend. "Something wonderful yet inexplicable was happening deep down inside me – something I'd never experienced before. My whole life unfolded before me as if projected on a screen. My mind was very clear. I saw myself as a child in the Sunday School class and heard the teacher say, 'Why not trust the Lord Jesus as your Saviour?' I saw the Salvation Army lassie singing on the streets of Paddington. I also saw the beds of shame and myself in the witches' covens. It dawned on my dark sinful heart that no one really loved me – not the men on the streets and in the Pubs, nor the Satanists and witches. Yet the singer said that the Lord Jesus cared and could take my sin and awful darkness away.

"Could it be true? Could it really be true that this Jesus really lived and really cared? Could He care for me, a common prostitute, drug addict and witch? If it were true, I would surely love Him in return. After years of shame and sadness, someone was reaching out to me – the tender Saviour who died in my place. For the first time in my life I felt dirty and thoroughly ashamed of the life I'd lived."

The evangelist preached that Christ could set anyone free who came to Him. He pleaded with his audience to turn from their sin (repent) and accept that Christ's death, as a substitute for sinners on the cross, was God's only means of salvation. The Lord Jesus was alive from the dead and those who knew their need of Him should immediately accept Him as Lord and Saviour. Doreen made a momentous choice that evening. Drawn by the love of the Lord she turned against Satan in her heart. Softly, through her tears, she prayed: "I want to come to You Lord Jesus – please take the darkness away."

When Doreen decided she wanted to be saved from sin and Satan, all hell broke loose. "That very night Lucifer stood by my bed. There was no mistaking him. I'd seen him often enough in the past and heard his voice many times. It was not imagination but very real indeed. 'You are mine', he said. 'You must obey me. Keep away from Christians, or you will die.' His form and face were black and twisted, his voice ugly with hate and threats. I tried to pray but it seemed useless. The power of evil was immense."

Doreen longed to have salvation from sin and deliverance from Satan. Her unique and special needs had become known to several mature Christians. One night they spent hours with her in an intense prayer battle for her complete deliverance. Through the mighty power of God the demons left Doreen and she was enabled by the Lord to completely turn from her former allegiances to Satan and trust in Him alone for salvation. What it says in the Bible was now true of her: "Delivered from the power of darkness, and translated into the kingdom of God's dear Son" (Col 1:13).

As of 2004 Doreen is still a living testimony to the delivering and transforming power of the gospel. She is proof that no pit it too deep that Christ cannot reach. In her own words: "I began to walk down many streets and found that they all led to degradation. The road to prostitution led to emptiness and guilt and utter loneliness, while the road to drug addiction led me eventually to prison. The darkest road of all led me to demon possession and near suicide. This was the road of witchcraft. Then in 1964, I heard of another road; the narrow road that leads to everlasting life. Could it be that one so wretched and vile as me would one day be transformed and walk the golden street arrayed in fine white linen, in that City of God? Yes, it was possible, wonderfully possible because Jesus Christ the Son of God died to redeem my soul from death and hell. At last I found the way, the true and living way through the Lord Jesus Christ who died in my place at Calvary.

"Human love is restricted and its ability to express itself is limited, but the love of God, which comes from above, is immeasurable. Human love can be debased by lust or it can deteriorate, or be degraded by jealousy or envy. In God's great love there is no darkness at all. There is no forgetfulness, no unfaithfulness and no disappointment. His love is unfailing."

To the Reader

Picture, if you will, an innocent boy being invited into an attractive room full of childish delights. Sweets, shiny toys, computer games and DVDs lie everywhere. Unrestricted, he engages in uncontrolled gratification of his every wish for hours on end. However, unknown to him, a sinister stranger has quietly locked the door behind him. Tired and feeling a creeping loneliness, the boy's thoughts turn to family and home. He tries the door, but in vain. As desperation sets in, his cries for help grow louder. Exhausted he slumps against the door as the room turns darker and colder with the passing of time. The tears begin to fall. How the discarded sweet wrappers and empty DVD cases mock him now! His mind is consumed with one thought – how to escape from his unexpected prison.

Spiritually speaking, a parallel pattern has been discernable in this book. Whether it was the attraction of angelic light, divination and crystals for Rachel; or wisdom and healing for Elka the Shaman; or knowledge in Egyptian magic for Lloyd Paul; or power for Audrey and Doreen – all were drawn into the magical world of witchcraft by spiritual forces acting as Pied Pipers, whose true motives initially remained concealed. In each case, after years of deep involvement in different forms of witchcraft, the time came when their eyes were opened to realise that the spell under which they had fallen, far from being benevolent, involved evil powers whose intentions were sinister.

To change the analogy, consider an onion. Before the core is reached, many layers must be peeled. While the promise of 'magic', spirituality, wholeness, enlightenment, knowledge of and ability to control the future are particularly appealing outer layers, few participants in the wide spectrum of 'the mystical' have any idea of the nature of witchcraft's inner core. Typically, peeling off the first layer may mean nothing more 'serious' than reading books about crystal healing, tarot, I Ching, yoga, astrology or channelling (spiritualism). Thousands of people first contact witchcraft through nothing more outwardly sinister than a workshop at a psychic fayre, a Halloween party or a fictional book involving various occult themes.

Frequently, due to the inbuilt curiosity of human nature, a hunger for more develops. Naturally a network of friends may quickly form with others who share similar interests. An invitation to join a group that meets regularly to study and explore spirituality soon peels back another layer. At some point Wicca is introduced to those who are ready for it and the commitment grows ever deeper.

Although many witches practise alone, large numbers of Wiccan recruits join covens. Core Wiccan practices and beliefs include goddess worship, respect for 'mother nature' and acceptance of the Wiccan Rede which states, "If it harm none, do what you will." Despite celebrating Halloween (which they call Samhain), invoking the aid of pagan deities and practicing ceremonial magic, no thought of 'Satanic' evil or malice enters many Wiccan minds. White witchcraft, they believe, is wholly positive and beneficial.

Some however, wish to remove further layers. Deeper wisdom, greater power, wider experience. Some rise to the top, leading local covens and speaking at workshops and seminars on occult themes. Watchful black witches are careful to spot talent and encourage eager Wiccans into darker magick, educating and persuading them to overcome inhibitions and accept practices previously considered 'wrong'. Willing adherents may be taken down a road that leads to Satanism and ultimately the core of it all – overt devil worship, with all its sordid practices.

Of course, not all witches follow that path. Many shrink from such a course – yet the potential is there. Some, with little moral conscience, plunge straight into black witchcraft and Satanism from the beginning (like Audrey and Doreen). Most, however, become slowly desensitised by degrees, just as a frog in a pan of water on a stove does not notice the rising temperature until it is too late.

One of witchcraft's essential beliefs is pantheism – the belief that everything is God. Ultimately this means that God is evil as well as good. Indeed, good and evil are understood as one and the same. Thus ancient deities from India and Greece are worshipped as 'gods' though they lie, commit adultery, steal, delude and use treachery. If a White Witch accepts this viewpoint, ignoring its fundamental logical inconsistency, there is little to prevent the crossover to black witchcraft (and ultimately Satanism) taking place, as this book's life stories show.

The ancient history of witchcraft tells of goddesses such as Artemis (Diana), Tanit, Astarte and Asherah who all demanded human sacrifice, especially that of infants. Even today, in cultures where witchcraft still dominates, millions live in fear of the 'spirits' and rely on their witchdoctors to appease them. White Witches perform an initiation ceremony using a white handled sacrificial knife called the 'Boleen'. It is used symbolically today amongst most covens, but its origin goes back to the days of literal human sacrifice. In 21st Century Western society, where existentialism and post-modernism hold sway (both of which deny absolute truth), multitudes of educated people are not prepared to agree – on philosophical grounds – that torturing babies is 'absolutely wrong' for all people, in all places at all times. There is no such thing as absolute truth – so they say (although this statement is an assertion of an absolute truth and therefore a contradiction in terms). A generation holding to this worldview that embraces witchcraft, will have little difficulty in justifying 'wrong' practices.

Many White Witches are unaware that their 'ancient' witchcraft Bible, the *Book of Shadows*, originated in the 1910s with Gerald Brousseau Gardner (1884–1964). Thus, Wicca is actually a modern Western religion. Though leading Wiccans such as Doreen Valiente and Margot Adler admit it, few Wiccans are aware that Wicca, in fact, "originated about 1939 with an Englishman, Gerald Gardner, who constructed it from the fanciful works of the self-styled magician [and noted Satanist] Aleister Crowley" (Witchcraft entry, Encyclopaedia Britannica, 2003).

The Bible teaches that the god of witchcraft is Satan. Subsequent to the eruption of his rebellious pride, this once beautiful and perfect angelic being suffered banishment from heaven (Isaiah 14:12-15). He became Satan, and the angels that followed him became the demons. Although known by White Witches as Lucifer and by some of the Black Witches as Satan, he is the same being, no matter how angelic he and his demons may appear. One of Satan's abilities, according to the Bible, is to transform himself into an angel of light (2 Corinthians 11:14).

By contrast, the creator God of the Bible is "light, and in Him is no darkness at all" (1 John 1:5). How utterly different to a mere 'force' with a light and dark side! The true God is righteous and holy. He has a holy name, sits on a holy throne and dispenses holy commandments. He has not, will not and cannot compromise with sin – such would be against all that God is.

God's creatures – men and woman – originally created sinless and in His image, have rebelled against God and cannot now even live up to their own standards. The Wiccan Rede states, "If it harm none, do what you will"; yet not a single human being has ever perfectly kept this 'rule', never mind God's holy commandments. Men and women all lie, steal and covet. Sins like these harm others and oneself. Most importantly of all, all sin is against God Himself. "There is no difference, for all have sinned and fallen short of the glory of God" (Romans 3:23).

Sin is not simply what one does – but what one *is* by nature. It is a condition of heart common to the entire human race. Our first parents sinned in the Garden of Eden and thus the whole human race was condemned to be born 'in sin' (Romans 5:19). Recognising 'indwelling sin', people have, for thousands of years, tried to conquer the problem and earn forgiveness by various systems of religion, ritual, self-works and self-righteousness.

Among pagans and witches there exists an endless array of methods through which solutions to human 'problems' are sought, from very legalistic rituals to psychotherapies, Reiki, crystal and psychic remedies. Since the actual 'sin problem' is not recognised it cannot be dealt with. Sin is against God and to effectively 'deal with it' God's holy demands

44

against sin must be met. His justly outraged righteousness against the rebellion and unbelief of mankind has to be appeased with a satisfactory payment.

Trying to satisfy God's demands by self-effort is doomed to failure, because the best that can be presented to God by men and women has already been declared as "filthy rags" by God Himself (Isaiah 64:6). All religious and ceremonial offerings are contaminated by the sinful nature and practise of the offerer. No one can be washed clean in dirty water. All of which goes to show that yoga, chanting, mantras, psychology and the like, cannot restore us to God.

The corrupt and rebellious heart of man gives Satan plenty of material on which to work. It more naturally drifts to sin than to righteousness. However, attractively packaged evil, which allures multitudes into the occult with promises of 'wisdom', wealth, health, power and fame, finally tricks its victim in the end as it leads them to an eternal hell, for "It is appointed unto men once to die but after this the judgment" (Hebrews 9:27).

Despite the rebellion of His creation, God intervened with a rescue plan by sending His sinless and only Son to the manger at Bethlehem. The virgin born Messiah, the Lord Jesus Christ, whose faultless life ended in death on the cross, came into the world to save sinners. That includes religious and non-religious people. It includes witches, both white and black. Perhaps mankind's highest concept of selfless love is illustrated each time someone lays down his life for a friend. God surpassed this – He laid down His life for his enemies in order to offer true peace, freedom, cleansing from sin and eternal life, based on His righteousness, not ours.

If you do not know Jesus Christ as your Lord and Saviour, now is the time to get right with God (whether you have been involved in witchcraft or not). This is what God requires of you:

1. Admit that you have sinned (fallen short of God's standards) and that you have broken His laws (e.g. by lying, stealing,

envying, lusting and practicing idolatry or self-sufficiency). Come to a proper sense of the dreadfulness of your sinful condition in the eyes of a holy and righteous God. Realise in the words of scripture that "Against You [God], You only, have I sinned, and done this evil in Your sight" (Psalm 51:4).

2. Forsake all self-righteousness, self-will and attachment to sin as the wilful pattern of your life. In other words, give up on your efforts to refine or reform yourself and let the truth of your helplessness, as well as your sinfulness, bring you to complete brokenness before your creator. Come to an end of self. As God says in His word: "Let the wicked forsake his way, and the unrighteous man his thoughts: and let him return unto the LORD, and he will have mercy upon him; and to our God, for he will abundantly pardon" (Isaiah 55:6). This includes involvement in witchcraft or any kind of occult activity such as divination, astrology, spiritualism, idolatry and sorcery, as mentioned in the Bible in Deuteronomy 18:9-14.

3. Come to the Lord Jesus now and receive Him as your Master and Saviour. By His death on the cross and His subsequent bodily resurrection from the dead, He has satisfied God's claim against sin. The wages of sin are death – but in the death of Christ, the debt sinners owed to God has been paid. The Bible declares: "He [the Lord Jesus] was wounded for our transgressions, He was bruised for our iniquities; the chastisement for our peace was upon Him, and by His stripes we are healed" (Isaiah 53:5)

God's wonderful promises, on which you can stake your whole eternity, are:

"Believe on the Lord Jesus Christ and you will be saved" (Acts 16:31)

"He who believes on the Son [Jesus] has everlasting life" (John 3:36)

When you repent and believe in Christ, God will give you His Holy Spirit, to be your guide, teacher and helper. He will lead you into all truth. The fruit of His work in your life will be love, joy, peace, patience, kindness, goodness, gentleness, faithfulness and self-control. He will never leave you but will daily equip you to cope with whatever trials and battles you will face.

If you have trusted Christ, start praying regularly to the Lord, thanking Him for blessings and asking Him for guidance and strength to turn away from temptation, and for help to live a true Christian life for His glory. Read the Bible each day, starting with the New Testament. Ask God to help you understand what you read and apply it practically to your life. Seek out a scriptural Bible believing church that believes the Bible is God's inspired Word and practises its principles of truth and love.

If you have been involved in the occult, you may experience spiritual attacks – but remember, Jesus Christ defeated Satan at the cross. The sin-atoning death of the Lord Jesus rendered Satan powerless to hold people in slavery (Hebrews 2:14). As a Christian you have Christ in you, and the Bible says, "He who is in you is greater than he who is in the world" (I John 4:4). Through the power of God's Word and fellowship with the Lord in prayer and worship, you will be able to "put on the complete armour of God, so as to be able to stand firm against all the stratagems of the Devil" (Ephesians 6:11).

"For by grace you have been saved through faith; and that not of yourselves, it is the gift of God; not as a result of works, that no one should boast" (Ephesians 2:8-9). "For God so loved the world, that He gave His only begotten Son, that whoever believes in Him should not perish, but have eternal life" (John 3:16).

If you would like confidential help or further information, please feel free to contact us. We can supply free Bibles, literature and details of Bible believing churches in your area. *If this book has been a help to you please let us know. We greatly value the feedback we receive from our readers.*

Published by:
Penfold Books
P. O. Box 26, Bicester, Oxon, OX26 4GL.
Tel: + 44 (0) 1869 249574
Fax: + 44 (0) 1869 244033
Email: penfoldbooks@characterlink.net
Web: www.penfoldbooks.com

Also available:

Dawn of the New Age	*5 New Agers Relate Their Search for the Truth*
Angels of Light	*5 Spiritualists Test the Spirits*
Messiah	*5 Jewish People Make The Greatest Discovery*
They Thought They Were Saved	*5 Born Again Christians Recall a Startling Discovery*
The Pilgrimage	*5 Muslims Make the Greatest Discovery*

Acknowledgements:
1. Thanks to Rachel Williams for personal permission kindly granted.
2. Thanks to Lloyd Paul Gallimore for personal permission granted.
3. The chapter called 'Shaman of the Rainforest' has been taken from the book *Christ's Witchdoctor* by Homer Dowdy, long out of print. If reprinting this abridged version has breached any existing copyright we apologise and pledge to honour any rights and permissions as soon as they are brought to our attention.
4. Excerpts from Audrey Harper's book *Dance With The Devil* have been used with the kind permission of the publisher, Kingsway Publications, Eastbourne, England.
5. Excerpts from Doreen Irvine's book *From Witchcraft to Christ* have been used with the kind permission of the publisher, Kingsway Publications, Eastbourne, England.